bistro

For Margot, Tristan and Phillipe.

Many thanks to Marine Labrune for her valuable and charming assistance. Many thanks as well to Jean and Alice who tasted many of these recipes and gave me their enlightened opinions.

Valérie Lhomme

The editor wishes to thank Édouard Collet, Christine Martin and Mélanie Joly for their valuable aid and Marine Barbier for her careful reading.

casual french cooking at home

bistro

Valérie Lhomme

Photographs by Jean-Blaise Hall
Design by Valérie Lhomme

[when the flavors blend...]

To everyone's delight, national borders are slowly disappearing in matters of cuisine. As the new century gets underway, we're witnessing a gradual acceptance of new culinary habits. We don't talk about "exotic cuisine" anymore because exotic means faraway, strange, and not necessarily authentic. We no longer consider Chinese, Indian or Mexican food to be unusual fare. The sources of inspiration for our cooking no longer matter as long as the results are delicious. It used to be that trying our hand at foreign cuisine was considered audacious, daring, but today it's part of our everyday lives. Ingredients that, in the past, had to be tracked with the skill of a detective or brought back by travelling friends, are now available locally from the neighborhood supermarket or even our corner grocer. We are no longer intimidated by peculiar spices, mysterious jars, or colorful fruits—but instead—we are learning how to use them. The world is coming to us and its flavors are being awakened in our kitchens. At the same time, we're discovering different ways of eating as well as dietary principles and eating habits from other countries. Our kitchens have become the melting pot for a natural blending of tastes; what was once quite curious is now so familiar that we forget its origins are foreign.

According to an entertaining but almost certainly false story, the word "bistro" was coined during the Napoleonic era, at which time Russian soldiers stationed in Paris would supposedly cry out "bistro!" ("quick!") when ordering drinks. In fact, it was more likely derived from terms used in Poitou or northern France. And just like its origin, the concept behind the word is somewhat vague. A bistro is a small restaurant, closely related to the "bouchons Lyonnais," a bar where the proprietor stands in the kitchen preparing the food for which Lyons is known. Italian trattorias, Spanish tapas bars and Greek tavernas are also relatives of the French bistro. Its identity rests with its decor, its service and its cuisine. Its interior includes banquettes covered with imitation leather, mirrors, etched glass signs, simple wooden chairs and marble-topped tables. Servers are impudent, amusing and fast, with or without mustaches, dressed in black with white aprons. The bistro mystique parallels that of the dance halls (guinguettes) and other places headed for extinction, where people go for nothing more than a little rest and distraction. The cuisine consists of standard dishes ordered from the menu, quickly served and quickly eaten. Actually, it's not much different from the cuisine normally associated with the French "bourgeois" or "homemade" tradition that has its roots in the rural exodus at the end of the nineteenth century. The coal merchant with his wines, and salt pork with lentils are as much the father of the bistro as the Alsatian brewer who came to Paris with his sauerkraut and snails. For the past twenty years or so, the bistro has been experiencing a revival. Many cooks as well as many fine chefs are striving to preserve this cuisine by reverting to the old recipes and adding their own innovative jewels of creativity to the traditional treasures. Follow their lead and recreate the bistro in your own home.

contents

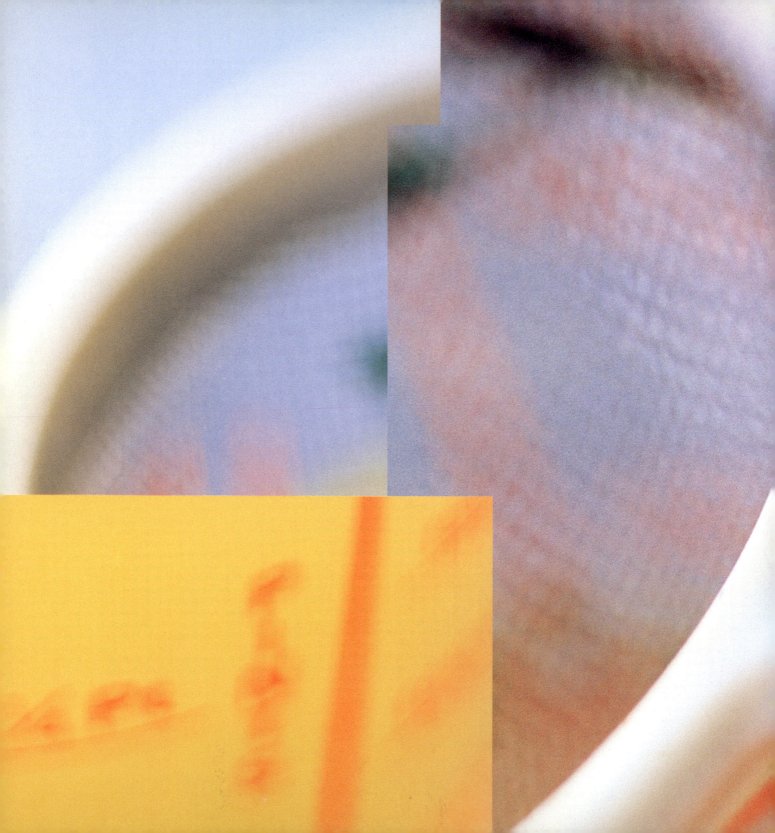

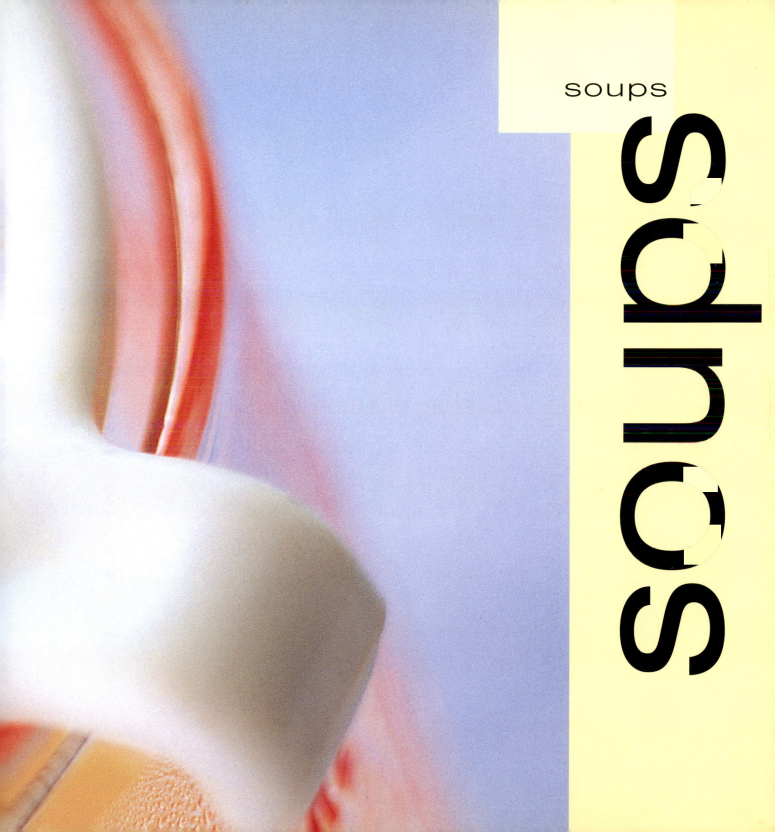

soups

soups

the tradition behind broth

When we were small, we dutifully picked at and played with the "soup that would make us big and strong." Now that we're grown and making our own choices we realize this is a pleasure, not a punishment…

As guardian of the ancient tradition of the all-important broth as the basis for much of French cuisine, the bistro refuses to abandon the family soup. Whether the famous onion soup, which revived revelers in the early morning hours around the Parisian dance halls, the fish soup that is everybody's favorite, or one of the newer more sophisticated versions, broth is here to stay.

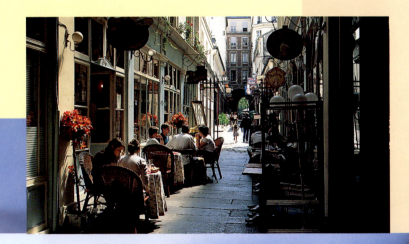

Serves 4–6
Prep time: 10 minutes
Cooking time: 30 minutes

1 pound onions
⅓ cup butter
Freshly ground pepper
1 pinch quatre épices*
2 teaspoons flour
6 cups poultry stock
  (see page 16)
Salt and freshly
  ground pepper
1 baguette
4 ounces grated Gruyère

* to make your own blend of quatre épices,
combine 1 tablespoon ground pepper, 2
teaspoons each of nutmeg and powdered
ginger and ½ teaspoon each of cinnamon
and cloves. There is no set recipe for this
spice mixture, so you can vary it as you wish.

[french onion soup]

Peel onions and cut into thin slices, then braise in butter for 15 minutes in a soup pot. Add pepper and a pinch of quatre épices, stirring occasionally to prevent them from becoming too brown.

When the onions are nice and golden, sprinkle with flour and stir to combine, add the stock, cover and simmer for 30 minutes. Season to taste with salt and pepper. Cut the baguette into rounds and toast them lightly.

Transfer the soup to bowls, and float several toasted baguette slices on top and sprinkle with grated Gruyère. Brown under a broiler immediately before serving.

[provençal vegetable soup with pesto]

Serves 4–6
Prep time: 30 minutes
Cooking time: 2 hours

2 zucchini
2 potatoes
1 pound navy beans
1 pound shelled fava beans
    (or 3 pounds unshelled)
¼ pound green beans
2 tomatoes
2 cloves garlic
1 onion
Several leaves of fresh basil
Kosher salt and freshly
    ground pepper
¼ pound spaghetti
2 ounces freshly grated
    Parmesan, additional

For the pesto:
1 tomato
1 bunch fresh basil
4 cloves garlic
¼ cup freshly grated
    Parmesan
¼ cup olive oil

Wash and chop zucchini. Peel, wash and dice potatoes. Shell the navy and fava beans (if unshelled). Peel the fava beans. Remove strings from green beans and cut into quarters.

Score tomatoes with the tip of a knife and blanch for 1 minute. Then plunge into cold water to stop the cooking process and peel. Remove the seeds and chop coarsely. Peel garlic and onion. Chop onion coarsely and crush garlic cloves with the flat side of a knife blade. Wash and dry basil.

Place all the vegetables in a large soup pot and cover with 2 quarts of water. Slowly bring to a boil. Add a small handful of salt, and pepper and let simmer for 1½ hours.

In the meantime, prepare the pesto. Blanch the tomato for 10 seconds, and plunge into cold water and peel. Remove the seeds and mash the flesh. Wash, dry and remove the leaves from the basil. Peel and remove sprouts from garlic cloves.

Combine these ingredients in a mortar, sprinkle with 2 ounces Parmesan and mash, while adding a thin stream of olive oil, until you have an oily paste.

Break the spaghetti in fourths and cook for 15 minutes in the soup.

Remove from heat, stir in the pesto, cover and wait a few moments before serving. Sprinkle with the additional Parmesan and serve immediately.

[vegetable soup with garlic croutons]

Wash, peel and chop carrots, leeks, turnips, celery root and potatoes. Cut bacon into cubes. Peel one garlic clove and the onion and mince. Wash, spin dry and chop almost all of the parsley, saving a few leaves for garnish.

In a large soup pot, melt 3 tablespoons of the butter. When it becomes foamy, add bacon and minced garlic and onion. Brown slightly, then add all the vegetables. Cover pot and braise several minutes. Add salt and pepper and cover with stock. Cover pot and simmer for 45 minutes.

When all the vegetables are cooked and tender, add chopped parsley and simmer for another 3 minutes. Then purée everything in a blender. Season to taste and add a little water if necessary. Keep hot.

In a frying pan, brown the slices of bread for 2 minutes on each side in the remaining butter. Then rub them with the remaining garlic clove and cut the bread into small cubes.

Serve the soup sprinkled with reserved parsley leaves and garlic croutons.

Serves 4–6
Prep time: 15 minutes
Cooking time: 45 minutes

½ pound carrots
½ pound leeks
½ pound turnips
¼ pound celery root
½ pound potatoes
¼ pound bacon
2 cloves garlic
1 onion
1 bunch Italian parsley
4 tablespoons butter
Kosher salt and freshly
  ground pepper
6 cups poultry stock
  (see page 16)
3 slices rustic French
  or Italian bread

Serves 4
Prep time: 20 minutes
Cooking time: 30 minutes

1 bunch fresh chervil
2 shallots
3 pounds kabocha squash*
3 tablespoons butter
2 teaspoons kosher salt
½ cup half-and-half
¼ teaspoon freshly
   ground cinnamon
Salt and freshly
   ground pepper

*acorn or another winter squash of
   about 3 pounds may be substituted

[winter squash soup with cinnamon]

Wash, dry and remove leaves from chervil and place in the refrigerator. Peel shallots and chop coarsely. Peel and remove seeds from squash and cut the flesh into small pieces.

In a large casserole, heat the butter. When it has melted, add the shallots and braise until translucent. Then add diced squash, salt and ⅔ cup water. Cover and simmer for 30 minutes.

Stir the squash purée thoroughly, and then fold in the half-and-half and cinnamon. Add more salt if necessary and turn the pepper mill several rotations over the top. Just before serving, remove from the heat and add bits of the chervil.

[potato soup with gruyère]

Serves 4
Prep time: 15 minutes
Cooking time: 20 minutes

2 pounds potatoes
   for mashing
Salt
4 ounces Gruyère
1 clove garlic
1½ cups whole milk
⅓ cup butter
1 pinch ground caraway
Freshly ground pepper

Peel and wash potatoes and cut into pieces. Sprinkle with salt and steam for about 20 minutes.

Grate cheese. Peel garlic and rub whole clove around the inside of a very heavy pot. Place the pot over low heat and add milk and butter. Heat until butter melts and mixture is very hot, but do not boil.

Purée potatoes in a food mill with a fine sieve and transfer to a large bowl. Gradually add hot milk mixture and whisk until foamy. Add a pinch of the caraway, half the grated Gruyère and pepper. Mix gently.

Serve very hot, gently reheating if necessary, topped with remaining Gruyère.

[poultry stock]

Wash and peel vegetables and chop coarsely. Put poultry carcasses and giblets in a stockpot and add 2 quarts water. Bring to a boil, remove scum, then add vegetables, and onion pierced with whole clove, bouquet garni, 1 small handful of salt and several peppercorns.

Simmer partially covered for 1½ hours. Strain stock. Cool thoroughly before refrigerating.

Makes 6 cups stock
Prep time: 10 minutes
Cooking time:
1 hour 40 minutes

2 carrots
1 leek
1 stalk celery
2 poultry carcasses
  with giblets
1 onion pierced with
  1 whole clove
1 bouquet garni (1 bay leaf,
  parsley stalks and 1 sprig
  fresh thyme; tied together
  with string)
Kosher salt and peppercorns

Makes about 10 wafers
Prep time: 2 minutes
Cooking time: 2 minutes

4 ounces freshly and
  finely grated Parmesan
1 tablespoon sifted flour

[parmesan wafers]

Combine finely grated Parmesan and flour. Place a small amount of this mixture in a nonstick frying pan and melt it over very low heat without letting it brown.

As soon as it begins to resemble lace, gently remove with a spatula and let cool over a rolling pin so that it takes on a curved shape.

You can prepare these wafers several hours ahead of time. They are delicious served with a glass of champagne or to tide you over until a full soup tureen arrives on the table.

[gazpacho with fresh goat cheese]

Bring a generous amount of water to a boil. Score the tomatoes with the tip of a knife and place in boiling water for 2 minutes. Remove the tomatoes and plunge into cold water to stop the cooking process. Peel the tomatoes.

Purée tomatoes in a food mill with a fine sieve (that will keep out the seeds). Gradually add the salt and olive oil. Refrigerate in a large bowl.

Coarsely chop the black olives. Cut cheese into thin slices. Wash, dry and snip the chives with scissors.

Before serving the gazpacho, add the ice cubes to "ice" it. Season to taste with salt and freshly ground pepper as necessary. Serve with olives, fresh cheese, chives and pepper from the pepper mill.

Serves 4
Prep time: 15 minutes

8 large ripe tomatoes
2 teaspoons salt
⅓ cup olive oil
8 black olives
1 fresh goat cheese
   (about 4 ounces)
1 bunch fresh chives
8 ice cubes
Freshly ground pepper

[eggs baked with chive-crème fraîche]

Preheat the oven to 350°F. Create a bain-marie (double boiler) by pouring boiling water into an ovenproof dish large enough to hold 4 ramekins (or whatever dish you are using for the food). Water should come about halfway up the sides of the ramekins. Place dish with water in the preheated oven. Butter 4 ramekins.

Pat dry and snip chive stems, combine with crème fraîche, add salt and pepper.

Break one egg in each ramekin, add a little of the chive cream and cook for 6 minutes in the bain-marie. Service with triangles of toasted bread for dipping.

Using the same principle, you can make eggs à la bourguignonne. In this case, you poach them in a sauce made of red wine, onions and chopped bacon and then cover them with this sauce. When served this way, these eggs will remind you that "soup" was originally composed of a slice of bread covered with stock, wine or sauce.

Serves 4
Prep time: 2 minutes
Cooking time: 6 minutes

1½ tablespoons butter
8 chive stems
4 teaspoons thick
   crème fraîche
Salt and freshly ground
   pepper
4 large extra-fresh eggs
Toasted bread triangles

To make a Polish-Jewish version of these chicken ravioli (kreplach), cook the chicken livers until pink and mince with some snipped chives. Add salt and pepper, mix well and use to fill the wonton skins.

[chicken soup with ravioli]

Salt and pepper the inside of a frying pan. Clean, wash and dry all the vegetables. Cut the celery into small sticks and bind up the leeks. Do not cut up carrots, turnips or onions.

In a large stockpot, bring poultry stock to a boil. Add bouquet garni, peppercorns and chicken. Bring to a boil once again, then simmer for 30 minutes. Do not boil the chicken because you don't want it to fall to pieces. Halfway through the 30 minutes, add the vegetables.

When the chicken is done, remove it from the stock and let cool. Remove the meat, chop it finely, and season to taste as necessary and bind it with the beaten egg.

Form small knobs of filling. Lay out the wonton skins on a lightly floured work surface. Place 1 knob of filling in the center of each square. Moisten the edges with a brush dipped in water and place a second square on top.

Use your fingertips to press the two squares together and cut off the excess dough using a pastry wheel. Repeat until all the filling has been used. Transfer the raviolis to a floured tray and cover with baking parchment.

Remove bouquet garni, peppercorns, onions and leeks from the stock. Dice the other vegetables, return to the stock and heat. Just before serving, put raviolis in boiling hot stock and cook for 4 minutes. Serve immediately.

Serves 4–6
Prep time: 35 minutes
Cooking time:
about 45 minutes

Salt and pepper
2 stalks celery
2 leeks
2 carrots
2 small turnips
2 onions
2 quarts poultry stock
  (see page 16)
1 bouquet garni
  (1 bay leaf, parsley stalks
  and 1 sprig fresh thyme;
  tied together with string)
5 peppercorns
1 chicken(about 3 pounds),
  cleaned
1 egg
1 package of wonton skins
  (Chinese ravioli)
Flour

[scallop soup]

Serves 4
Prep time: 30 minutes
Cooking time: 30 minutes

12 scallops
2 leeks
3 carrots
2 potatoes
1 small turnip
1 onion
1 stalk celery
5 sprigs Italian parsley
4 tablespoons butter
¼ pound chopped bacon
½ cup crème fraîche

For the concentrated
fish stock (fumet):
Several stalks parsley
1 sprig fresh thyme
1 bay leaf
1½ tablespoons butter
1 onion pierced with
1 whole clove
Kosher salt and freshly
ground pepper
½ cup dry white wine

Prepare the stock: Tie together the parsley stalks, thyme sprig and bay leaf to make a bouquet garni. In a casserole, melt the butter. When it becomes foamy, add scallop corals (if you have them), the onion pierced with a whole clove and the bouquet garni. Add salt, pepper, white wine and 4½ cups water. Simmer for 20 minutes over low heat.

In the meantime, wash leeks, removing wilted leaves, and cut into thin slices. Wash and peel carrots, potatoes, turnip and onion, then dice. Clean celery stalk and dice. Remove and wash parsley leaves.

In a casserole, melt the 4 tablespoons butter. When it becomes foamy, brown the bacon, then the vegetables. Braise until translucent and tender.

Strain the scallop fumet and pour it over the cut-up vegetables. Simmer for 5 minutes, then add parsley leaves and mix thoroughly.

Halve the scallops crosswise. Poach for 5 minutes in simmering soup. Season to taste as necessary.

Serve immediately, adding 2 tablespoons crème fraîche to each bowl.

[potato leek soup with parmesan]

After removing leaves that are wilted and very dark, wash leeks and cut into julienne strips. Peel and wash potatoes and cut into cubes.

In a large saucepan, melt butter. When it becomes foamy, add the leek strips and diced potatoes. Sauté slowly without browning. Add poultry stock and bring to a boil. Lower the heat and simmer for 20–30 minutes, depending on size and tenderness of vegetables.

Remove a small amount of potato, purée and return to the soup. Add salt, pepper and half the Parmesan, mix well and season to taste as necessary. Transfer soup to bowls and sprinkle with remaining Parmesan.

Serves 4
Prep time: 20 minutes
Cooking time:
about 25 minutes

3 leeks
5 baking potatoes
3 tablespoons butter
1 quart poultry stock
 (see page 16)
Salt and freshly
 ground pepper
⅓ cup freshly grated
 Parmesan

[split-pea soup]

Put split peas in a bowl with 2 quarts of water and soak for 1 hour. Peel garlic, remove sprouts and crush cloves.

Rinse split peas and put in a saucepan. Cover with stock, add garlic and bouquet garni and salt and bring to a boil. Remove scum and simmer partially covered for 1 hour.

Cut bread into small cubes and fry in 3 tablespoons of the olive oil. Strain croutons.

Remove bouquet garni and purée split peas in a food mill with a fine sieve. Thin the purée with water or stock. Add salt and pepper as necessary.

Serve topped with the remaining tablespoon of olive oil and garnish with croutons and parsley leaves.

Serves 4
Soaking time: 1 hour
Cooking time: 1 hour

6 ounces split peas
2 cloves garlic
1 quart poultry stock
 (see page 16)
1 bouquet garni
 (1 bay leaf, parsley stalks
 and 1 sprig fresh thyme;
 tied together with string)
1 teaspoon kosher salt
2 large slices of rustic
 French or Italian bread
¼ cup fruity olive oil, divided
Kosher salt and freshly
 ground pepper
Fresh Italian parsley leaves

Cut chile peppers in half and remove seeds. Crush in a mortar along with garlic that has been peeled and has sprouts removed, and add salt and saffron, until it becomes a paste.

If you use a potato, mash it with a fork and add it and the sandwich bread to the spicy paste. Continue pounding and stirring while adding olive oil and fish fumet. The sauce should become thicker.

Serve with fish soup (see page 28).

Serves 4
Prep time: 10 minutes

2 small fresh chile peppers
3 cloves garlic
1 pinch kosher salt
4 saffron threads
1 cooked potato (optional)
1 slice white bread
3 tablespoons olive oil
¼ cup concentrated fish
  stock (fumet, see page 68)

[rouille]

a spicy provençal sauce to accompany fish

Fish soup is an ever popular dish, whether it tastes of the

south of France as in the recipe below or takes on more of

an oceanic flavor. It can be found on every coast, from the

Mediterranean to the North Sea, but is also a common

sight on the tables of bistros in large cities. To get the

most out of this dish, don't forget garlic cloves to rub on

the warm croutons and a glass of cold white wine.

[mediterranean fish soup]

Ask your fish vendor to fillet the fish and give you the trimmings. Wrap the trimmings in cheesecloth and set aside.

Clean leek, carrots and celery and cut into small pieces. Peel and mince onion, shallots and garlic cloves. Remove seeds from chile pepper.

Prepare the bouquet garni. Score tomatoes with the tip of a knife, plunge into boiling water for 2 minutes and peel. Remove seeds and chop coarsely.

In a large stockpot, heat oil and sauté garlic, onion and shallots. Add chopped vegetables, tomatoes, salt and pepper, then cover with fish fillets and trimmings. Add about 1 quart water, the bouquet garni and chile pepper and simmer for 20 minutes over low heat.

Remove the cheesecloth containing the fish trimmings, and the bouquet garni. Purée soup in a blender and season to taste. Add saffron and simmer for an additional 10 minutes.

Serve immediately with toasted croutons and the rouille.

Serves 4
Prep time: 20 minutes
Cooking time: 40 minutes

1 rockfish or perch or
  striped bass (about
  5 pounds)
1 leek
2 carrots
1 stalk celery
1 onion
3 shallots
2 cloves garlic
1 red chile pepper
1 bouquet garni
  (1 bay leaf, parsley stalks
  and 1 sprig fresh thyme;
  tied together with string)
1 pound tomatoes
½ cup olive oil
Salt and freshly
  ground pepper
1 jar saffron
Toasted croutons, rouille
  (see page 26) for garnish

Serves 4
Prep time: 20 minutes
Cooking time: 15 minutes

2 pounds celery root
1 large potato for mashing
1 tablespoon kosher salt
1 pinch freshly
   grated nutmeg
1 tablespoon olive oil
1 teaspoon hazelnut oil
$1/3$ cup crème fraîche
Salt and freshly
   ground pepper
8 thin strips bacon
Fresh leaves from
   1 stalk celery

[cream of celery root soup with fried bacon]

Peel, wash and dry celery root and potato and cut up into small pieces. Bring to a boil 1¼ cups water with the salt, add the vegetables and simmer for 15 minutes until tender. Test doneness by piercing them with the tip of a knife.

Purée vegetables in a food mill with a fine sieve, adding enough of the vegetable water to make a creamy soup. Add nutmeg, both types of oil and crème fraîche and stir. Add a little salt and pepper. Keep warm.

In an ungreased, nonstick frying pan, brown bacon strips on both sides. Transfer cream of celery to bowls, garnish each bowl with 2 strips of crisp bacon and a few celery leaves, and serve immediately.

entrées

entrées

salads at the bar

Whether savored at the counter or eaten at the marble-topped tables, these traditional first courses take on new life when flavored with currently popular seasonings such as dill, pistachio nuts and soy sauce. At the same time, the bistro jealously guards its ancestral secrets: The art of correctly proportioned vinaigrettes, terrines, pressed meats, marinated fish, and composed salads, which are a small meal in themselves.

Serves 4
Prep time: about 20 minutes

3 very white endives
4 tablespoons olive oil
2 tablespoons walnut oil
2 tablespoons sherry vinegar
Salt and freshly
  ground pepper
5 ounces bleu d'Auvergne
  or Stilton cheese
4 ounces shelled
  unsalted pistachios

[endive salad with toasted pistachios]

Detach leaves and wash and dry endives. Prepare the vinaigrette by mixing together the two types of oil, vinegar, salt and pepper without emulsifying them too much. **C**rumble the cheese.

In an ungreased, nonstick frying pan, toast the pistachios for 3 minutes. Cut endive leaves in half and dress with vinaigrette. Top with cheese, and hot pistachios. **S**erve immediately.

[spinach salad with haddock and dill]

Serves 4
Prep time: 15 minutes

½ lemon
1 lime
1 bunch fresh dill
1 pound haddock
4 large handfuls of
    spinach greens
4 tablespoons olive oil
2 teaspoons pistachio
    or hazelnut oil
Salt and freshly
    ground pepper

Squeeze juice from the ½ lemon and the lime separately. Wash, dry and snip dill. Cut haddock into thin slices and cover with lime juice. Sprinkle with half the dill and set aside. Gently wash and spin dry spinach greens.

Prepare the vinaigrette by combining the two types of oil, lemon juice, a small amount of salt and pepper. (Salt very sparingly since haddock is already salted.)

Dress spinach salad, then transfer to bowls. Garnish with sliced haddock and remaining dill. Serve immediately.

[pressed rabbit with tiny vegetables]

Ask your butcher to cut the rabbit into small pieces and give you the liver and kidneys.

Peel onions and carrots. Wash carrots and slice crosswise. Wash and dry tarragon and remove leaves. Peel garlic clove.

In a casserole, melt butter. When it becomes foamy, add rabbit pieces, onions, thyme, garlic and bay leaf. Season with salt and pepper. Brown slowly, then add wine. Crumble and add the half cube of chicken bouillon and simmer for 30 minutes. Then add carrots, peas and the rabbit liver and kidneys and continue cooking for about 10 more minutes.

When the rabbit is done, bone it, cut meat into thin slices and cut the offal into small pieces. Remove thyme, bay leaf and garlic, then strain stock and reduce for 5 minutes over high heat.

Soften gelatin powder in ¼ cup cold water. Add softened gelatin to hot stock that has been removed from the heat. Add tarragon leaves.

Line a 9 x 13-inch pan with plastic wrap. Arrange boned rabbit slices and vegetables in the pan, gradually pouring in stock. Fold over plastic wrap, pack down by placing a small board and weight on top. Refrigerate for 12 hours before serving. Serve with tarragon mayonnaise, gherkins or onion chutney (see page 37).

Serves 4
Prep time: 30 minutes
Cooking time: 40 minutes
Refrigeration time: 12 hours

1 rabbit with liver
  and kidneys
4 ounces pearl onions
4 young carrots
½ bunch fresh tarragon
1 clove garlic
3 tablespoons butter
1 sprig fresh thyme
1 bay leaf
Salt and freshly
  ground pepper
2 cups dry white wine
½ cube chicken bouillon
1 small handful fresh
  shelled peas
2 teaspoons powdered
  gelatin

3 large tart apples
½ lemon
1 bunch muscat grapes
1 small handful
  fresh arugula
1 small bunch fresh cilantro

For the vinaigrette:
2 tablespoons grapeseed oil
1 tablespoon toasted
  sesame oil
1 tablespoon olive oil
1 tablespoon Japanese
  soy sauce
1 tablespoon wine vinegar
2 pinches Chinese
  five-spice powder
Salt and freshly
  ground pepper

1 smoked duck breast
  fillet, sliced

[smoked duck fillet, apple and grape salad]

Wash apples, core and slice thinly. Sprinkle sparingly with lemon juice to prevent discoloration. Wash grapes and separate from stalks. Wash arugula and cilantro and spin dry.

Prepare vinaigrette by mixing the different types of oil, and then add soy sauce, wine vinegar and five-spice powder. Season with salt and pepper.

On each plate, arrange alternate layers of smoked duck fillet and apple slices. Garnish with a little arugula, cilantro and a few grapes. Dress with vinaigrette and serve.

[onion chutney]

Serves 4
Prep time: 10 minutes
Cooking time: 30 minutes

2 pounds onions
½ cup dry white wine
1¼ cups brown sugar
1 small cinnamon stick
1 whole clove
¼ cup crème de cassis

Peel onions and cut into thin round slices.

In a saucepan, bring white wine and brown sugar to a boil.

Add sliced onions, cinnamon stick, whole clove and crème de cassis.

Simmer for 30 minutes over low heat, stirring occasionally.

Pour mixture into a canning jar and store several days in the refrigerator.

This condiment is excellent with poultry, cold white meats and terrines.

[chicken liver terrine with port]

Clean chicken livers thoroughly and remove all traces of gall. Put bacon and chicken livers through a mincer with a fine cutter, or purée in a food processor.

Combine and beat crème fraîche, egg yolks, port and quatre épices. Season with salt and pepper. Add bacon and chopped livers and stir until the mixture becomes creamy. Season to taste as necessary.

Preheat oven to 350°F and create a bain-marie by pouring boiling water into an ovenproof dish large enough to hold a terrine of about 2 cups. Place the dish with water in the preheated oven.

Wash and dry bay leaves. Place 1 leaf on the bottom of the terrine. Cover with chicken liver mixture and place the other leaf on top. Bake for 40 minutes in the oven in the bain-marie. Let terrine cool completely before refrigerating.

Serves 4
Prep time: 20 minutes
Cooking time: 40 minutes

12 ounces chicken liver
8 ounces bacon
½ cup crème fraîche
3 egg yolks
2 tablespoons port
1 pinch quatre épices
  (see page 11)
Salt and freshly ground pepper
2 bay leaves

Serves 4
Prep time: 10 minutes
Refrigeration time: 30 minutes

12 fresh sardines
Salt
1 shallot
2 large purple onions
1 small bunch fresh dill
1 small bunch fresh chives
1 small bunch fresh cilantro
2 lemons
½ cup fruity olive oil
Freshly ground pepper
4 slices bread, toasted
1 clove garlic, peeled

[raw sardines marinated in herbs]

Ask you fish vendor to clean, scale and fillet the sardines. Rinse and dry in a cloth. Lay them flat on a large plate and sprinkle with salt.

Peel shallot and onions. Wash and dry herbs. Coarsely chop herbs and shallot. Cut onions into thin round slices. Squeeze juice from lemons and combine lemon juice with olive oil. Add herbs, shallot, onions and pepper.

Pour mixture over sardines, cover with plastic wrap and refrigerate for 30 minutes before serving. Serve with toasted bread rubbed with garlic.

[gherkins and pearl onions in vinegar]

Scrub gherkins and place in a deep dish. Cover with salt and let set 24 hours.

The next day, peel pearl onions. Wash gherkins in water and dry one by one. In a saucepan, bring water to a boil. Place tarragon sprig in boiling water for a few seconds to blanch it, then cool and dry it. Peel garlic cloves and cut in half.

Place gherkins, white onions, tarragon, garlic and all the seasonings in the jar. Cover with white vinegar and seal tightly. Allow to cure for at least 6 weeks before serving.

The longer you wait, the better they will become. But be careful not to keep them for more than a year.

Makes 1 large jar
(or 4 small jars)
Prep time: 30 minutes
Curing time: 6 weeks

2 pounds gherkins
Kosher salt
10 ounces pearl onions
1 sprig fresh tarragon
2 cloves garlic
1 teaspoon coriander seeds
1 teaspoon mustard seeds
½ teaspoon peppercorns
2 whole cloves
1 sprig fresh thyme
1 quart white vinegar

[parisian mushrooms with a lemon-flavored cream]

Trim stems and wash mushrooms quickly under running water. Dry and slice thinly lengthwise, sprinkling with a bit of the lemon juice as you go, to prevent discoloration.

Combine crème fraîche with the remaining lemon juice, lime juice, quatre épices, ginger and salt and pepper. Add quatre épices and ginger. Stir first, then gently fold in mushrooms. Refrigerate until you're ready to serve.

Serves 4
Prep time: 10 minutes

1¼ pounds mushrooms,
   white and firm
Juice of 1 lemon
½ cup crème fraîche
Juice of 1 lime
1 teaspoon quatre épices
   (see page 11)
⅛ teaspoon ground ginger
Salt and freshly
   ground pepper

This first course became popular in Parisian bistros during the 1970s.

It originally called for Chavignol cheese, browned for a longer period of time.

For this recipe you can always serve it sliced.

[warm goat cheese salad]

Serves 4
Prep time: 15 minutes

4 large small handfuls
  mâche (lamb's lettuce)
2 tart apples
4 rounds of small, creamy
  goat cheese, such as
  rocamadours
1 teaspoon fresh thyme
Salt and freshly
  ground pepper

For the vinaigrette:
3 tablespoons olive oil
2 tablespoons peanut oil
1 tablespoon walnut oil
2 tablespoons
  balsamic vinegar
12 pecan halves
Salt and freshly
  ground pepper

Wash mâche several times, being careful to remove all sand.

Wash apples and remove core and seeds. From each apple, cut two large round slices ½ inch thick where the diameter is widest. Place one cheese on each slice, sprinkle with a little thyme and 1 pinch salt and turn pepper mill one rotation over the top.

Transfer apples with goat cheese to a dish and slide them under the broiler. Broil for 3 minutes, just long enough for the goat cheese to brown, making sure they don't spread out too much.

Prepare the vinaigrette by mixing the different types of oil and vinegar, and seasoning with salt and pepper. Dress mâche, transfer to plates, add pecan halves and place apples with goat cheese on top. Serve immediately.

[the vinaigrettes]

"classic" vinaigrette

1 gray shallot
2 tablespoons wine or sherry vinegar
3 tablespoons sunflower oil
3 tablespoons olive oil
Salt and freshly ground pepper

Peel and chop shallot and combine with vinegar. Then add all oil, stirring constantly. Season with salt and pepper. This vinaigrette is perfect for dressing the lettuce.

To dress a Chinese salad, replace 1 tablespoon sunflower oil with toasted sesame oil and add a little soy sauce.

For a warm scallop salad, reduce the amount of vinegar and preferably use a mixture of fine oils (such as pistachio, hazelnut or walnut).

herb vinaigrette

¼ cup olive oil
2 tablespoons sunflower oil
1 tablespoon finely chopped Italian parsley
1 tablespoon finely chopped fresh tarragon
3 tablespoons lemon juice
Salt and freshly ground pepper

Mix the different types of oil and chopped herbs, then add lemon juice. Season with salt and pepper. This vinaigrette is especially suitable for spicing up cold fish or crisp vegetables.

tapenade vinaigrette

3 tablespoons balsamic vinegar
1 tablespoon black-olive tape-nade (Provençal black olive paste)
6 tablespoons olive oil
Salt and freshly ground pepper

Combine balsamic vinegar and tapenade. Add olive oil, while stirring constantly. Season sparingly with salt and add pepper. This vinaigrette goes with slightly bitter salads such as radicchio and is an ideal complement to warm leeks.

If you store oils and vinegars in a cool place, away from sunlight, you can keep them for a long time. Don't hesitate to keep a wide variety on hand so you can vary your recipes and adapt your choices to whatever dish is being served.

[mussels in white wine with curry]

Scrape and wash mussels. Peel shallots and chop coarsely. Wash, dry and chop Italian parsley. In a large stockpot, melt the butter. When it becomes foamy, add shallots and half the curry powder. Simmer gently 2–3 minutes, while stirring constantly.

Add white wine, bouquet garni and the mussels. Add bouquet garni, cover and simmer over high heat until the mussels open, shaking the pot occasionally. When all the mussels are open, remove pot from heat and strain the stock. Keep mussels in a bowl covered with a plate.

Reduce stock to half the amount over high heat, and then add remaining curry, parsley and crème fraîche. Let boil a few seconds. Season to taste as necessary with pepper. Add mussels, carefully pour creamy sauce over the top and serve immediately.

Serves 4
Prep time: 15 minutes
Cooking time: 15 minutes

2 quarts mussels
    (3–4 pounds)
2 large shallots
6 sprigs Italian parsley
3 tablespoons butter
1 tablespoon curry powder
½ cup dry white wine
1 bouquet garni
    (1 bay leaf, parsley stalks
    and 1 sprig fresh thyme;
    tied together with string)
¼ cup crème fraîche
Freshly ground pepper

[herring and potatoes in oil]

Serves 4
Prep time: 10 minutes
Cooking time:
about 15 minutes

1½ pounds boiling potatoes
3 large sweet onions
1 shallot
½ bunch Italian parsley
Salt
¼ cup peanut oil
Freshly ground pepper
8 herring fillets in oil

Peel and wash potatoes. Peel and cut onions into round slices. Peel and mince shallot. Wash and dry parsley, remove leaves and chop coarsely.

Place potatoes in the basket of a steamer, sprinkle with salt and cover with onion slices. Steam for about 15 minutes, depending on their size. Test doneness by piercing each one with the tip of a knife. They should remain slightly firm.

In a large salad bowl, combine oil, shallot and parsley. Turn pepper mill four rotations over the top and add herring.

When potatoes and onions are done, immediately combine with herring and serve immediately.

The potatoes must be served warm. If you buy herring in oil, and not vacuum-packed, use the herring oil to season the potatoes.

[goat cheese in olive oil]

Serves 4
Prep time: 10 minutes
Curing time: 1 week

2 sprigs fresh thyme
2 sprigs fresh savory
1 sprig fresh rosemary
1 fresh spicy red
   chile pepper
2 cloves garlic
1¼ cup very fruity olive oil
4 rounds small, creamy
   goat cheese, such as
   rocamadours
Several peppercorns

Gently wash and dry herbs and pepper. Peel garlic cloves.

Pour olive oil in a jar with a lid. Add herbs, pepper, garlic, cheeses and peppercorns. Cover and seal tightly. Store in refrigerator, cure for one week, serve with crusty French or Italian bread or arugula salad.

The cheeses must not be ripe. After several days in the oil, they will become spicy.

Serves 4
Prep time: 15 minutes
Cooking time:
about 15 minutes
Refrigeration time: 1 hour
Curing time: 48 hours

For the marinade:
2 sprigs fresh thyme
2 sprigs fresh rosemary
2 bay leaves
1 clove garlic
¾ cup olive oil
1 teaspoon pink
   peppercorns (may
   substitute black
   peppercorns)
1 teaspoon black
   peppercorns

1 organic lemon
Salt
1 clove garlic
1 sprig fresh thyme
1 sprig fresh rosemary
1 bay leaf
1 fresh tuna steak
   (about 1 pound)
Salt

[tuna in oil]

Prepare the marinade: Wash and dry thyme, rosemary and bay leaf. Peel garlic. Pour olive oil over these seasonings. Add half the pink peppercorns and half the black peppercorns and steep for 24 hours.

The next day, cut the lemon into round slices and cover with salt. Refrigerate for 1 hour.

Peel garlic. Wash and dry herbs. In 1 quart salted water, combine herbs with garlic and the remaining black and pink peppercorns. Bring to a boil and place the tuna in this court bouillon. Remove from heat and let cool.

Sponge off steak, and remove skin and bones and place in a jar with a lid. Add lemon slices after removing salt. Cover with marinade, close jar and refrigerate for 24 hours before serving. Do not keep more than 3 days.

fish

fish

fresh bistro fish

Fish served in bistros is known for its modesty. Why limit yourself to fine and expensive fish when you could make equally good use of salt cod, whiting, calamari, skate, cod and mackerel? Nevertheless, these simple, tasty, quick dishes yield the best results only when the fish is very fresh.

Serves 4
Prep time: 10 minutes
Cooking time: 30 minutes

1 perch (aka porgy)
  or sea bream (about
  2½ pounds), cleaned
1 bunch fresh thyme
3 pounds coarse salt

[sea bream in a salt crust]

Rinse fish under running water.

Preheat oven to 400°F. Wash and dry thyme, reserving 2 large sprigs. Crumble the rest and mix with salt.

On an ovenproof dish, arrange a layer of salt about ½ inch thick. Insert reserved thyme sprigs inside fish cavity. Transfer the fish to the dish and completely cover with the remaining salt. Pack down the salt to form a sealed and even crust. Bake for 30 minutes in the oven.

Just before serving, break the crust and remove the few stray grains of remaining salt. Remove skin and serve fillets immediately seasoned with a warm vinaigrette (see page 45).

[small red bell peppers stuffed with salt cod]

Place salt cod in a colander in cold water, skin side up, and soak 12 hours, changing the water several times.

The next day, wash and dry bell peppers. Remove stalks and seeds without breaking them apart. Wash and dry chile pepper. Score tomatoes with the tip of a knife, plunge into boiling water for 1 minute, then plunge into cold water and peel. Remove seeds and mash the flesh. Wash, dry and remove leaves from the bunch of basil. Set aside several leaves for garnish and coarsely chop remaining leaves. Peel garlic and mince.

In a casserole, heat 2 tablespoons of the olive oil. Add bell peppers, cover and gently simmer for 10 minutes; set aside.

In unsalted boiling water, poach cod for 5 minutes and break apart layers of meat. In the casserole, brown the cod with mashed tomato flesh, minced garlic and 2 tablespoons of the olive oil. Remove from the heat and add chopped basil and chile pepper.

Stuff each little bell pepper with spiced cod. Pack in the filling, being careful not to tear the pepper. Arrange all the stuffed peppers in a gratin dish, sprinkle with remaining olive oil, cover with aluminum foil and bake for 15 minutes in the oven at 350°F.

During the last moments of cooking, uncover and sprinkle stuffed bell peppers with freshly grated Parmesan. Serve garnished with fresh basil leaves.

This dish is delicious either hot or cold. If cold, serve with a few black olives and an arugula salad.

Serves 4
Prep time: 20 minutes
Cooking time: 35 minutes
Soaking time: 12 hours

1 pound salt cod
12 small red bell peppers
½ red chile pepper
2 tomatoes
½ bunch fresh basil
1 clove garlic
8 tablespoons olive oil,
   divided (½ cup)
¼ cup freshly
   grated Parmesan

[marinated tuna and stewed fennel]

Cut tuna steak into eight pieces, removing the backbone and skin. Refrigerate. Peel, remove sprouts and coarsely chop 3 of the garlic cloves and the onions. Scrub lemon and lime under running water. Remove rind from half the lime and half the lemon and chop finely. Then squeeze juice from lemon and lime. Wash, dry and remove seeds from chile pepper and chop finely. Peel and grate ginger.

Combine all these ingredients with sesame oil and 4 tablespoons of the olive oil. Add salt and pepper and pour mixture over tuna pieces. Cover with plastic wrap. Refrigerate for 1 hour, occasionally turning over fish pieces.

Wash and dry fennel bulbs and cut into round slices ½ inch thick. In a casserole, heat remaining olive oil. Add fennel and remaining garlic clove (peeled and coarsely chopped). Brown at a high temperature for several seconds, then add 2 tablespoons water. Add salt, pepper and the saffron. Cover and simmer for 30 minutes. Add a little water during the cooking process, if necessary.

Preheat oven to 350°F.

Place tuna in a shallow baking dish and cover with its marinade. Bake for 10–15 minutes in the oven, occasionally turning over the pieces. When the fish is done, remove it from the dish and keep warm between two plates.

Wash, dry, and remove leaves from cilantro. Boil marinade for 3 minutes to reduce it slightly, add fresh cilantro and cover the tuna with the sauce. Serve immediately with stewed fennel.

Serves 4
Prep time: 15 minutes
Marinating time: 1 hour
Cooking time:
40–45 minutes

1 tuna steak
   (about 1¼ pounds)
4 cloves garlic, divided
2 onions
1 lemon
1 lime
1 fresh red chile pepper
1 piece ginger root
   (about ½ ounces;
   the size of a kumquat)
1 tablespoon toasted
   sesame oil
6 tablespoons
   olive oil, divided
Salt and freshly ground
   pepper
4 bulbs fennel
1 jar saffron
½ bunch fresh cilantro

Serves 4
Prep time: 30 minutes
Cooking time: 40 minutes

1½ pounds small calamari
1 bunch fresh dill
6 cloves garlic, divided
4 ounces black olives
16 cherry tomatoes
2 cups brown rice
5 tablespoons
  olive oil, divided
Salt and freshly
  ground pepper
1 tablespoon tapenade

[calamari stuffed with rice and dill]

Ask your fish vendor to clean the calamari without opening them and to give you the tentacles. Wash them and dry carefully with a cloth.

Wash, dry and chop dill. Peel and finely chop garlic cloves. Pit and coarsely chop olives. Wash tomatoes. Rinse rice under running water.

In a nonstick frying pan with high sides, heat 2 tablespoons of the olive oil. When the oil is hot, slowly sauté half the garlic and dill, then the rice. Cover with water and add salt and pepper. Simmer for 30 minutes, while stirring occasionally. Add a little water during the cooking process, if necessary.

When the rice is tender, remove from heat and add remaining dill, tapenade and black olives. Stuff each calamari with this mixture, then close with a wooden toothpick.

In the frying pan, heat the remaining olive oil. Sauté the remaining garlic, tomatoes and then the calamari and tentacles. Add salt and pepper and simmer for about 10 minutes over low heat until slightly golden and translucent. Serve immediately with a small mesclun salad.

[herb brandade]

salt cod purée

Place salt cod in a colander in cold water, skin side up, and soak for 12 hours, changing the water several times.

The next day, peel potatoes and cook in boiling salted water (using 2 teaspoons salt per quart of water). Wash, dry and chop dill and parsley. Peel and crush garlic and combine with 5 tablespoons of the olive oil.

Cut salt cod into several pieces and poach for 10 minutes in simmering water (unsalted!). Strain, remove skin and bones and break apart layers of meat. Peel potatoes and mash in a ricer. Add salt cod and herbs, then add garlic olive oil, while stirring constantly with a wooden spoon. Season with salt and pepper if necessary. Spread in a gratin dish. Add remaining olive oil and reheat a few moments in an oven heated to 350°F.

Serves 4
Prep time: 20 minutes
Soaking time: 12 hours
Cooking time: 30–40 minutes

1¼ pounds salt cod
2 pounds potatoes (for mashing)
1 bunch fresh dill
½ bunch Italian parsley
2 cloves garlic
6 tablespoons olive oil, divided
Salt and freshly ground pepper

Serves 4
Prep time: 10 minutes
Cooking time: 20–30 minutes

2 pounds potatoes
  (for mashing)
½ cup crème fraîche
½ cup olive oil
Salt and freshly
  ground pepper

[potato purée
with olive oil]

Peel and wash potatoes. In a large saucepan, cook in boiling salted water (using 1 tablespoon salt per quart of water). Test doneness by piercing each one with the tip of a knife. When tender, strain and mash potatoes in a ricer. Add crème fraîche and mix thoroughly. While stirring constantly with a wooden spoon, add olive oil in a thin stream. Season to taste with salt and pepper.

Serve this purée with roasted fish.

[eggplant, zucchini and tomato tian]

layered vegetable pâté

Wash and dry eggplant, zucchini, tomatoes and thyme. Peel garlic cloves, remove sprouts and coarsely chop. Cut vegetables into round slices about ½ inch thick. Preheat oven to 400°F.

Arrange eggplant slices in a gratin dish* in an overlapping pattern. Sprinkle with chopped garlic, thyme, salt and pepper and cover with part of the olive oil. Then cover with alternating slices of tomato and zucchini. Cover with the remaining olive oil. Season with salt and pepper and bake for 30 minutes in the oven at 400°F. Turn heat down to 350°F and bake for another 30 minutes.

This tian is excellent either hot or cold and is a delicious accompaniment to grilled fish or a confit of shoulder of lamb (see page 79).

*A shallow dish used for baking and serving.

Serves 4
Prep time: 10 minutes
Cooking time: 1 hour

1 large eggplant
1 large zucchini
3 large tomatoes
2 sprigs fresh thyme
2 cloves garlic
Salt and freshly
  ground pepper
¼ cup olive oil

[cod steak]

Wash and dry bay leaves. Peel, wash and dry potatoes and slit them without cutting all the way through. Preheat oven to 350°F.

Arrange potatoes on a gratin dish and place 1 bay leaf inside each one. Sprinkle with half of the butter, cut into bits. Add white wine and 2 tablespoons water. Season with salt, turn the pepper mill five rotations over the top and cover with aluminum foil. Bake for 25 minutes in the oven at 350°F. Then remove foil and bake for another 10 minutes.

Grease a nonstick frying pan with ⅓ of the remaining butter and sear the cod pieces, skin side down. Lower heat and cook for 8 minutes.

Remove skin from the cod pieces, transfer to a serving plate; season with salt and pepper. Slowly melt the remaining butter. Pour melted butter over them and serve with the bay leaf potatoes.

Serves 4
Prep time: 15 minutes
Cooking time:
45–50 minutes

12 bay leaves
  (fresh if possible)
12 medium-sized
  potatoes
8 tablespoons butter
¼ cup dry white wine
Salt and freshly
  ground pepper
4 thick cod fillets about
  5 ounces each, with
  the skin

For this recipe, look for authentic Scottish haddock—whole smoked haddock fillet—which has an incomparable taste. It's smaller than the orange-tinged cod generally sold under the name of haddock.

[haddock with cabbage and garlic cream]

Wash, dry and crumble thyme. Remove wilted leaves from cabbage. Remove stalk, while keeping leaves joined together as much as possible. Blanch cabbage for 5 minutes in a large amount of boiling water. Strain, detach leaves and cut them into strips. Place them in the basket of a steamer, sprinkle with fresh thyme and steam for 20 minutes.

Wrap unpeeled garlic cloves in baking parchment and bake for 15 minutes in the oven at 350°F. Peel and mash them with a fork and mix with crème fraîche, a little salt and pepper and the quatre épices. Set aside.

Bring milk to a boil and add haddock. Poach over low heat, making sure the milk does not come to a boil again.

Warm garlic cream over low heat. Add lemon juice, while stirring with a whisk. Season to taste if necessary.

Strain and serve haddock with cabbage and covered with garlic cream.

Serves 4
Prep time: 15 minutes
Cooking time 50 minutes

1 sprig fresh thyme
½ head savoy cabbage
4 cloves garlic
½ cup crème fraîche
Salt and freshly ground
   pepper
2 pinches quatre épices
   (see page 11)
1 quart whole milk
1¼ pounds haddock
Juice of ½ lemon

[skate with grilled bell peppers]

Serves 4
Prep time: 30 minutes
Cooking time: 30 minutes
Marinating time: 30 minutes

1 clove garlic
1 shallot
6 tablespoons
olive oil, divided
2 red bell peppers
1 yellow bell pepper
3 tablespoons
balsamic vinegar
Salt and freshly
ground pepper
1½ pounds skate
2 tablespoons
pickled capers

Peel and mince garlic and shallot. Cover with a bit of the oil.

Wash and dry bell peppers. Arrange on a baking sheet under the broiler and broil for about 15 minutes. Turn them as soon as one side of the skin blackens so that all sides are uniformly broiled. Place bell peppers in a large bowl, seal tightly with plastic wrap and wait for 10 minutes. This time is essential because it helps to detach the skin. You will then see how easy it is to peel the bell peppers. Cut them in half lengthwise inside the bowl (so as not to lose the juice). Remove stalks and seeds and then peel.

Cut peppers into strips. Add balsamic vinegar, the remaining olive oil, garlic and shallot, and salt and pepper. Let steep for 30 minutes in a warm place.

Preheat oven to 400°F.

Cut skate in half and place in a gratin dish. Add ½ inch water and bake for 10–15 minutes in the oven, depending on the skate's thickness.

In the meantime, strain off the pepper marinade and pour into a saucepan. Add capers and warm over low heat.

When the skate is done, quickly carve off the fillets and transfer them to very hot plates. Season with salt and pepper. Add peppers, and cover with hot marinade and serve.

If you don't know how to carve the skate fillets, cut the raw fish into four sections, cook it and serve it as is.

[red mullet roasted with garlic]

Ask your fish vendor to scale and clean the mullets. Keep the very tasty livers (located behind the head) and put them back in the fish.

Wash and dry tomatoes and rosemary. Peel and remove sprouts from garlic cloves and cut into quarters. Cut tomatoes in half and arrange them in a gratin dish with the cut sides up. Embed ½ garlic clove and a bit of rosemary in each one. Sprinkle with sugar, pour on 4 tablespoons of the olive oil and add salt and pepper. Bake for 1 hour in the oven at 400°F. If necessary, reduce oven temperature toward the end.

Slice baguette. Toast slices and rub with 1 garlic clove, then cover with tapenade.

In a large nonstick frying pan, heat the remaining 2 tablespoons of olive oil and the last garlic clove. Reduce heat and fry mullets for 3 minutes on each side. Season with salt and pepper. Serve immediately with tomatoes, and croutons topped with tapenade.

Serves 4
Prep time: 10 minutes
Cooking time: approx.
1 hour 10 minutes

8 red mullets weighing
  3–4 ounces each
16 small, very
  ripe tomatoes
1 sprig fresh rosemary
10 cloves garlic
1 teaspoon
  granulated sugar
6 tablespoons olive
  oil, divided
Salt and freshly
  ground pepper
½ baguette
⅓ cup black
  olive tapenade

[sauce vierge with herbs]

Wash, dry and chop basil and parsley. Peel, remove sprouts and mince garlic. Squeeze juice from half the lemon.

Score tomatoes with the tip of a knife and place in a saucepan of boiling water for 2 minutes. Then plunge into cold water, peel, remove seeds and mash flesh.

In a double boiler combine the mashed tomato and olive oil. Add salt, pepper, herbs and garlic and simmer for 10 minutes. Just before serving, add lemon juice.

This simple and flavorful little sauce can be served with any grilled or poached white fish.

Serves 4
Prep time: 10 minutes
Cooking time: 10 minutes

½ bunch fresh basil
4 sprigs Italian parsley
2 cloves garlic
½ lemon
2 tomatoes
6 tablespoons olive oil
Salt and freshly
  ground pepper

Peel onion, carrot and garlic. Remove strings from celery stalk. Pierce onion with whole clove. Bind together herbs for bouquet garni.

Place all these ingredients in a stockpot. Add a small handful of salt and 6 peppercorns. Then add white wine, 1½ quarts water, and fish trimmings and bones, and bring to a boil. Simmer for 30 minutes over low heat, then strain through a fine-mesh sieve.

You can use this flavorful stock to poach fish, or freeze it in ice-cube trays and use it as a base for sauces.

Makes 1½ quarts stock
Prep time: 10 minutes
Cooking time: 30 minutes

1 onion
1 carrot
1 clove garlic
1 stalk celery
1 whole clove
1 bouquet garni
  (1 bay leaf, parsley stalks
  and 1 sprig fresh thyme;
  tied together with string)
Salt
Peppercorns
1¼ cups dry white wine
2 pounds bones and
  trimmings from lean fish

[fish fumet]

concentrated fish stock

Sardines in oil have long been considered the quintessential back-up hors d'oeuvre. Originally a simple and practical solution for preserving fish, they are now a favorite dish that true sardine aficionados allow to age for years in order to enhance their flavor. This melt-in-your-mouth, oily little fish with its lustrous bronze hue is the pride of Brittany (which produces the best) and deserves to be called "confit de sardines" (preserved sardines).

[salmon with bacon]

Wash and lightly salt salmon steaks. Wrap each salmon steak in two slices of bacon and secure with two wooden toothpicks. Refrigerate. Wash, dry and finely chop rosemary. Peel, wash and dry potatoes, and grate coarsely and combine with rosemary, salt and pepper.

In a large nonstick frying pan, melt half of the butter. Add potatoes and press them down with the flat of your hand to form a galette (potato pancake). Cook for 5 minutes over low heat and turn the galette. Add the remaining butter and cook the other side. Carefully brown the potato pancake, turning it over several times.

Place the salmon wrapped in bacon under the broiler, on the center oven rack. Broil for 15 minutes, stopping to turn over halfway through. Cut the potato pancake into quarters. Place one bacon-wrapped salmon steak on each potato pancake quarter and serve.

Do not grate the potatoes ahead of time because they blacken very quickly. On the other hand, you can precook the galette and finish cooking it, while you cook the salmon.

Serves 4
Prep time: 20 minutes
Cooking time: 35 minutes

4 skinless salmon steaks
  (about 5 ounces each)
Salt
8 thin slices bacon
1 sprig fresh rosemary
8 medium-sized potatoes
⅓ cup butter
Freshly ground pepper

[mackerel with mustard]

Wash and dry mackerels. Smear inside of fish with about half of the mustard and refrigerate for 30 minutes.

Reduce fish fumet until a bit thickened, add crème fraîche while whisking, then add remaining mustard. Season to taste with salt and pepper.

Arrange mackerels in a gratin dish, cover with half the sauce and place under broiler. Broil for 5 minutes, then remove the dish from the oven, turn the fish, cover with the remaining sauce and place under broiler for another 5 minutes.

Serve with potato purée with olive oil (see page 59).

Serves 4
Prep time: 10 minutes
Cooking time: 10 minutes
Refrigeration time:
30 minutes

8 small mackerels or young
  spring mackerels, cleaned
3 tablespoons Meaux
  (or other grainy) mustard
½ cup fish fumet
  (see page 68)
½ cup crème fraîche
Salt and freshly
  ground pepper

Serves 4
Prep time: 10 minutes
Cooking time:
40–50 minutes

2 carrots
1 onion
1 clove garlic
1 whole clove
1½ cups green lentils
    (about 12 ounces)*
¼ pound thick sliced bacon
1 bouquet garni
    (1 bay leaf, parsley stalks
    and 1 sprig fresh thyme;
    tied together with string)
Salt
4 salmon pieces (about
    5 ounces each), with skin
¼ cup olive oil, divided
Freshly ground pepper

*Any lentils may be substituted

[roast salmon with green lentils]

Peel and slice carrots. Peel onion and garlic and pierce onion with whole clove.

Rinse lentils and place in a saucepan. Cover with a generous amount of water and add carrots, onion, garlic, bacon and bouquet garni. Bring to a boil, then simmer partially covered for 30 minutes. Add salt 10 minutes before lentils are done cooking (they should remain slightly firm). Place fish (skin side down) under the broiler and broil for 5 minutes. Turn, skin side up, and continue broiling until opaque all the way through (about 5 additional minutes, depending on thickness).

Strain lentils and remove bouquet garni and onion. Remove and dice bacon, then brown diced bacon in 2 tablespoons of the olive oil. Add lentils, stir and keep warm.

Remove broiled skin from salmon pieces. Season with salt and pepper, sprinkle with remaining olive oil and serve on a bed of lentils.

meat

meat

rare or medium

It's no coincidence that the most renowned bistros of Paris and the provinces are located near the old markets or slaughterhouses. Many of the markets have disappeared but the bistros remain, kept going by devoted carnivores. Times have changed and market porters no longer come into the bistros dressed in their red aprons to rest their elbows on the bar. But we can still have skirt steak with shallot sauce, beef with carrots or grilled pig's feet.

[chateaubriand with pepper]

Serves 4
Prep time: 15 minutes
Cooking time: 15 minutes

2 pounds potatoes for frying
Sunflower oil
4 beef fillets (about
   6 ounces each)
2 teaspoons coarsely
   ground pepper
3 tablespoons butter
¼ cup veal or chicken
   bouillon (instant)
2 tablespoons crème fraîche

Peel potatoes and cut into fries. Fry in hot oil and drain when they rise to the top.

Roll beef fillets in pepper. In a nonstick frying pan, heat butter and sear meat for 3 minutes on each side. Remove from the pan and set aside.

Preheat oven to 300°F. Deglaze the frying pan with veal bouilon. Add crème fraîche and the remaining pepper. Thicken over low heat. Season to taste with salt.

Place Chateaubriands in the oven for 5 minutes. Submerge fries in oil once again until golden. Serve meat covered with sauce and accompanied by fries.

Chateaubriands should be cooked at a slightly lower temperature than steaks of normal thickness in order to prevent the formation of a "crust," which would keep the heat from reaching the center.

[pot-au-feu]

Wash vegetables and peel and trim as appropriate. Pierce each onion with 1 whole clove. Cut turnips, carrots, potatoes and celery into quarters. Cut greens off leeks and bind the white parts together with a string.

Remove marrow from bones and soak marrow in cold water for 2 hours.

Cut meat into large pieces and place in a large stockpot. Cover with cold water and bring to a boil. Cook for 40 minutes at medium heat. Carefully skim off scum from stock to remove fat and all impurities. When there is no more "white foam," add coarse salt, bouquet garni, black peppercorns, onions and leek greens. Simmer for about 2 hours, occasionally removing scum.

Now add all the vegetables, except the cabbage. In a large saucepan, blanch cabbage separately in boiling water and then add to stock. Cook for 20 minutes, add marrow and cook for about 10 minutes longer.

Remove bouquet garni and leek greens. Serve meat surrounded by vegetables and bathed in stock. Garnish with salt, freshly ground pepper, mustard, and gherkins and pearl onions in vinegar.

Serves 4
Prep time: 45 minutes
Soaking time: 2 hours
Cooking time: 2½ hours

2 leeks
2 turnips
2 onions
2 carrots
1 pound potatoes
¾ pound green cabbage,
    cut in wedges
2 stalks celery
2 whole cloves
4 marrow bones
¾ pound short ribs
¾ pound shoulder
    of beef (chuck)
Coarse salt
1 bouquet garni
    (1 bay leaf, parsley stalks
    and 1 sprig fresh thyme;
    tied together with string)
10 peppercorns
Salt and freshly
    ground pepper
Mustard
Gherkins and pearl onions
    in vinegar (see page 40),
    on the side

[three-meat and potato casserole]

Cut meats into pieces. Peel and chop onions. Wash, dry and chop parsley. **I**n a casserole, heat olive oil. Sauté meats and onions with spices. Add salt and pepper. Sprinkle with a little of the parsley. Lower heat, cover and simmer for 30 minutes, adding a little water if necessary.

In the meantime, cook potatoes in boiling salted water. Bring milk to a boil. When potatoes are done, drain and mash in a ricer, gradually adding boiling milk and 6 tablespoons of the butter. The purée should be coarse and a little firm.

Coarsely chop meats with a knife and add the remaining parsley, meat juices and onions. Season to taste and spread out the entire mixture in a small gratin dish. Cover with the potato purée. Sprinkle with bits of butter and bake for 20 minutes in the oven at 350°F. Serve with a green salad.

This dish is traditionally made with leftover meat that has already been cooked.

Serves 4
Prep time: 20 minutes
Cooking time: 50 minutes

¾ pound boneless lean veal
¾ pound boneless lean
  pork scallop
¾ pound boneless
  lean lamb
2 large onions
1 bunch Italian parsley
3 tablespoons olive oil
2 pinches freshly
  grated nutmeg
1 pinch cumin
Salt and freshly
  ground pepper
2 pounds potatoes
  (for mashing)
½ cup whole milk
8 tablespoons butter,
  divided

[shoulder of lamb confit*]

Serves 4
Prep time 10 minutes
Cooking time: 2½ hours

1 sprig fresh thyme
1 sprig fresh rosemary
1 boneless shoulder of lamb
   (about 3 pounds)
2 tablespoons olive oil
1 teaspoon harissa (a spicy
   Middle Eastern/North
   African condiment)
Salt and freshly ground
   pepper
12 shallots
8 cloves garlic

Preheat oven to 350°F. Wash and dry thyme and rosemary. Smear meat with olive oil and harissa, and sprinkle with salt and pepper. Place lamb in an earthenware dish with the herbs. Cover with aluminum foil and bake for 1 hour in the oven.

Peel shallots. After lamb has been cooking for 1 hour, add shallots and add the garlic cloves with the peels on. Cover and lower temperature to 300°F. Bake for another hour, occasionally basting the lamb with its juices.

Remove aluminum foil and let shoulder brown for about 30 minutes. Serve with eggplant, zucchini and tomato tian (see page 60) or some stewed tomatoes The longer and more slowly the lamb cooks, the better it will be.

*Confit is a process of preserving meat or poultry by cooking it in its own fat

[potato gratin]

Serves 4
Prep time: 20 minutes
Cooking time:
1 hour 15 minutes

1¼ pounds potatoes
¼ pound comté or Gruyère
1 clove garlic
3 tablespoons
   softened butter
3 pinches freshly
   grated nutmeg
1⅓ cups crème fraîche
Salt and freshly
   ground pepper

Peel potatoes. Cut into very thin round slices, rinse under running water and dry in a cloth. Grate cheese.

Rub the inside of a gratin dish with peeled garlic clove and then grease with butter. Combine nutmeg and crème fraîche, and season with salt and pepper.

Preheat oven to 350°F and prepare a bain-marie large enough for the gratin dish (see page 18).

Pour a little of the crème fraîche in the gratin dish. Line the bottom with a layer of potatoes. Season with salt and pepper and add a little cheese. Repeat these layers until the potatoes have all been used, and top with a layer of crème fraîche (reserve a bit of cheese and a bit of crème fraîche).

Place in the oven and bake for about 1 hour in the bain-marie. Sprinkle with the remaining cheese and top with the remaining crème fraîche. Bake for another 10 minutes in the oven.

[glazed carrots with orange]

Peel, wash and dry carrots, and cut into round slices. Cut orange in half and squeeze out juice.

In a sauté pan, sauté carrots in butter, and add orange juice and then add just enough water to cover carrots. Add cumin, sugar, salt and several rotations of the pepper mill.

Simmer for about15 minutes until the carrots have absorbed all the liquid and are glazed.

Serves 4
Prep time: 5 minutes
Cooking time: 15 minutes

2 pounds young carrots
1 orange
2 tablespoons butter
1 pinch cumin
1 teaspoon
  granulated sugar
Salt and freshly
  ground pepper

Prep time. 10 minutes

¼ cup butter
1 bunch fresh tarragon,
  parsley, chives or cilantro,
  as desired

[herb butter]

Begin by working the butter into a paste using a wooden spoon.

Wash, dry, and finely chop the herb selected. Combine with softened butter at a ratio of 1 part butter to 1 part chopped herb.

To prepare shallot or garlic butter, follow the same procedure, blanching garlic cloves or shallots ahead of time. Use a lower ratio of garlic.

Refrigerate these mixed butters. You can cut them up just before serving fish, grilled meat or steamed vegetables.

[rack of lamb on a bed of potatoes]

Serves 4
Prep time: 20 minutes
Cooking time: 1 hour

2 pounds potatoes
2 pounds onions
½ cup butter, divided
2 racks lamb (6 ribs each)
Salt and freshly
  ground pepper
1 bay leaf
1 sprig fresh thyme

Peel, wash and cut potatoes into thin round slices. Place in a bowl of cold water. Peel onions and slice thinly. In a frying pan, melt 2 tablespoons of the butter. When it becomes foamy, sauté onions over low heat and then remove from heat.

Season racks of lamb with salt and pepper. Wash and dry herbs.

Preheat oven to 400°F.

Butter the bottom of a large casserole and arrange a layer of potatoes on the bottom. Sprinkle with onions, thyme, salt and pepper. Add bay leaf and dot with butter. Cover with a second layer of potatoes. Repeat this process until no ingredients remain, cover and bake for 30 minutes in the oven.

Place racks of lamb on potatoes, fat side down. Bake for 15 minutes, uncovered, in the oven. Turn meat over and cook for 15 minutes longer. Let stand 10 minutes before serving.

[zucchini gratin]

Serves 4
Prep time: 10 minutes
Cooking time: 15 minutes

2 pounds zucchini
1 clove garlic
2 tablespoons olive oil
1 pinch freshly grated
  nutmeg
Salt and freshly
  ground pepper
½ cup crème fraîche
¼ pound freshly
  grated Parmesan

Wash and dry zucchini and cut into round slices. Peel, remove sprouts and mince garlic.

In a sauté pan, heat olive oil. When hot, sauté zucchini. Add garlic, nutmeg, salt and pepper.

Simmer for about 15 minutes over low heat until the vegetables are translucent.

Thoroughly mix crème fraîche, Parmesan and zucchini. Pour into a dish and brown top for 3 minutes under the broiler.

For this simple recipe, select a young domestic rabbit with flexible joints. To peel the onions, you can submerge them for several seconds in boiling water. Serve with the Riesling you used for cooking.

[rabbit in white wine]

Peel onions and garlic. Cut bacon into small pieces. In a casserole, brown bacon in 1 tablespoon of the butter.

Flour rabbit pieces. Remove bacon and onions from casserole and sauté rabbit pieces, liver and kidneys. Flambé with cognac. Set aside liver. Season rabbit with salt and pepper. Add bouquet garni and Riesling to casserole. Cover and simmer for 30 minutes. Add bacon, onions and liver and simmer for another 20 minutes.

In the meantime, cut off the ends of the mushroom stems and wash the mushrooms rapidly under running water. Dry and slice thinly. In a frying pan, sauté mushrooms in remaining butter until all the liquid has evaporated. Then add to rabbit and simmer for 10 minutes.

Remove rabbit pieces and mushrooms, discard bouquet garni and reduce stock until thickened. Add crème fraîche, season to taste with salt and pepper and simmer for 5 minutes. Cover rabbit and mushrooms with this sauce and serve with steamed new potatoes.

Serves 4
Prep time: 15 minutes
Cooking time: 1 hour

½ pound pearl onions
2 cloves garlic
½ pound bacon
4 tablespoons butter, divided
4 teaspoons flour
1 large rabbit, cut into pieces with liver and kidneys
2 tablespoons cognac
Salt and freshly ground pepper
1 bouquet garni (1 bay leaf, parsley stalks and 1 sprig fresh thyme; tied together with string)
2 cups Riesling
1 pound cultivated mushrooms
½ cup crème fraîche

[veal rolls stuffed with olives*]

Serves 4
Prep time. 30 minutes
Cooking time: 40 minutes

4 veal scallops (about
5 ounces each)
1 cup green olives
(about 4 ounces)
10 sprigs fresh cilantro
1 sprig fresh lemon thyme
1 egg
5 ounces boneless pork,
finely chopped
5 ounces boneless veal,
finely chopped
Salt and freshly ground pepper
1 preserved lemon, available at
specialty stores (see glossary)
3 tablespoons butter
$\frac{1}{8}$ teaspoon veal or chicken
bouillon (instant)
$\frac{1}{3}$ cup dry white wine
1 bouquet garni (1 bay leaf,
parsley stalks and 1 sprig
fresh thyme; tied together
with string)

Ask your butcher to flatten the scallops.

Pit and chop olives. Wash, dry and remove leaves from 5 of the cilantro sprigs and from the thyme. Beat the egg.

Combine chopped meats with herbs, egg and about half of the olives. Add salt and pepper and form into 4 balls of filling. Place each ball in the center of a flattened scallop and roll the meat, so as to firmly enclose the filling. Tie together with string.

Cut preserved lemon into quarters. Melt butter in a large skillet or Dutch oven. When it becomes foamy, brown remaining olives and the veal bundles on all sides. Add salt and pepper. Sprinkle with veal bouillon and add white wine. Add bouquet garni and cover. Simmer for about 30 minutes over low heat, moistening with a little water, if necessary.

Add preserved lemon quarters and simmer veal for another 10 minutes. Sprinkle with snipped cilantro and serve immediately with fresh noodles or steamed new potatoes.

*If available, use vertes cassées, which are cracked green olives soaked in salt water and flavored with fennel. They are a specialty of Nice.

[beef with carrots]

Cut up beef. Wash, dry and remove leaves from parsley. Peel carrots, onions and garlic. Chop onions coarsely. Cut carrots into thick round pieces. Remove sprouts from garlic and crush.

In a large skillet or Dutch oven, heat the butter and oil. Add onions and slowly brown. Set aside.

Lightly flour beef pieces, then sear in the casserole. Add crushed garlic. Season with salt and several rotations of the pepper mill, then moisten with red wine and meat bouillon. Add onions, bouquet garni, several parsley leaves and whole clove, cover and simmer for 2 hours over low heat.

Add carrots to casserole and simmer for another hour.

When meat is tender, remove meat pieces and carrots from the casserole. Strain sauce and reduce a few moments over high heat. Season to taste with salt and pepper. Add the remaining parsley and cover beef and carrots with sauce. Serve immediately.

Serves 4
Prep time: 20 minutes
Cooking time: 3 hours

2 pounds beef chuck
½ bunch Italian parsley
2 pounds carrots
2 onions
2 cloves garlic
2 tablespoons butter
2 tablespoons peanut oil
4 teaspoons flour
Salt and freshly ground
   pepper
2 cups red wine
2 cups meat bouillon
   (instant)
1 bouquet garni
   (1 bay leaf, parsley stalks
   and 1 sprig fresh thyme;
   tied together with string)
1 whole clove

Ask your butcher to cut up the chicken, separating the legs from the thighs and cutting breasts into two pieces.

Peel and dice zucchini. Wash and remove leaves from tarragon. Peel and crush garlic. In a large casserole, melt butter and brown chicken with bacon, garlic and curry. Add salt, pepper, half the tarragon and the diced zucchini. Cover and simmer for 30 minutes, stirring occasionally. Add giblets and simmer for 15 minutes.

Remove chicken pieces from the casserole and keep them warm. Add crème fraîche and the remaining tarragon to chicken juices. Let boil a few moments and season to taste with salt and pepper.

Bring a large saucepan of salted water to a boil. Cook tagliatelle until al dente, then add to sauce. Serve immediately.

Serves 4
Prep time: 10 minutes
Cooking time: 50 minutes

1 free-range chicken with
   giblets (about 3 pounds)
1 zucchini
½ bunch fresh tarragon
1 clove garlic
3 tablespoons butter
5 ounces bacon,
   coarsely chopped
½ teaspoon curry powder
Salt and freshly
   ground pepper
½ cup crème fraîche
12 ounces fresh tagliatelle
   pasta (fresh if available)

[tarragon chicken]

Whether prepared in a casserole or roasted, free-range

chickens should always be large. Whether white or yellow,

their meat should be firm and elastic, their legs long

and their thigh bones slightly curved, indicating that

they were able to run free. Any seasonings can be used,

but by far the best are tarragon, thyme, lemon, garlic

and bay leaves.

[duck breast in salt]

Make lattice incisions across breast fat. Rub with coarse salt and set aside. Peel potatoes and celery root and coarsely chop.

In a large saucepan, bring salted water to a boil (at a ratio of 4 teaspoons of salt per quart of water) and cook potatoes and celery root until tender. Test doneness by piercing vegetables with the tip of a knife. Drain vegetables and purée in a food mill with a coarse sieve. Add butter, half of crème fraîche and a little milk. Season to taste. Add nutmeg and set aside.

Preheat broiler. Arrange breasts with the skin side up on a rack with a pan underneath to catch the fat. Broil breasts in the center of the oven for 8 minutes, turn them and broil for another 8 minutes. Finish by browning them, skin side up, 4 minutes longer. Cover with aluminum foil and set aside. The meat should be pink and tender.

Bring the remaining crème fraîche to a boil and add pink peppercorns, quatre épices, salt and pepper. Carefully reheat purée, adding enough of the remaining milk to reach desired consistency.

Cut breasts into thin slices (quickly so they don't cool) and transfer them to plates. Add celery root-potato purée, cover with crème fraîche-peppercorn sauce and serve immediately.

To prevent unpleasant odors when cooking the breasts, fill the dish, catching the fat with water. This will keep it from burning.

Serves 4
Prep time: 15 minutes
Cooking time: 20 minutes

2 duck breasts
Coarse salt
1½ pounds potatoes
   (for mashing)
1 pound celery root
¼ cup butter
½ cup crème fraîche,
   divided
⅓ cup whole milk
1 pinch freshly
   grated nutmeg
1 teaspoon pink
   peppercorns
2 pinches quatre épices
   (see page 11)
Salt and freshly
   ground pepper

Serves 4
Prep time: 10 minutes
Cooking time: 1½ hours

15 fresh bay leaves
24 cloves garlic
1 large free-range chicken,
  with giblets cleaned but
  not trussed (about
  3 pounds)
Salt and freshly ground
  pepper
¼ cup butter

[chicken stuffed
with bay leaves]

Preheat the oven to 400°F. Wash and dry bay leaves. Remove the first layer of peel from the garlic cloves but do not peel completely.

Generously season inside of the chicken with salt and pepper. Insert bay leaves, 16 of the garlic cloves and the giblets. Tie legs together with string. Place chicken, breast side up, in a large casserole and smear with softened butter. Season with pepper. Add remaining garlic cloves and place the chicken in the oven.

After 30 minutes lower oven temperature to 350°F. Turn chicken to prevent breast from drying out and let it cook in the meat juices. Turn chicken breast side up after 45 additional minutes. Cook for 15 minutes longer.

Before serving, remove bay leaves. Crush garlic cloves and mix with meat juices. Remove garlic and giblets from inside the chicken and serve.

desserts

desserts

how about a little dessert?

There is little difference between bistro desserts and those made by your grandma. Both are simple, both are intended to please, both are scented with vanilla and cinnamon. The menu is traditional—apple tart, pears in wine, crème anglaise (custard sauce), and rich, flourless chocolate cake. These dishes always bring back sweet recollections of former times that we want to keep with us forever.

Serves 4
Prep time: 10 minutes
Cooking time: 35 minutes
Refrigeration time:
at least 1 hour

1 quart whole milk
1 vanilla bean
1 small stick cinnamon
1 cardamom pod
¾ cup short-grain rice
2 tablespoons preserved
  orange rind
2 egg yolks
⅓ cup granulated sugar

[spiced rice pudding with preserved fruit]

Boil milk with vanilla bean split open lengthwise, cinnamon and cardamom.

Place rice in a saucepan, cover generously with water and bring to a boil for 1 minute. Drain and return to saucepan.

Remove cinnamon from milk and pour milk over rice. Simmer for 30 minutes, stirring occasionally.

Finely dice preserved orange rind. Beat egg yolks with sugar until mixture lightens, then carefully fold in rice. Add orange rind and cook for 5 minutes.

Remove vanilla bean. Let cool completely before refrigerating. Serve chilled.

[crème au caramel]

baked caramel custard

Preheat oven to 350°F and prepare a bain-marie (see page 18) in a dish large enough to hold 8 ramekins.

In a small saucepan, melt 3 tablespoons of the sugar to make a light-gold caramel. Pour into the ramekins.

Bring whole milk to a boil. Beat whole eggs and yolks with remaining sugar until mixture lightens, then add boiling milk. Mix gently and pour into the ramekins. Set ramekins in the bain-marie and place in the oven. Bake for 30 minutes.

Let cool completely before refrigerating. Serve in ramekins or turned out onto a plate.

Makes 8 small custards
Prep time: 10 minutes
Cooking time: 20 minutes
Refrigeration time:
at least 1 hour

½ cup granulated
   sugar, divided
2 cups whole milk
2 eggs
4 egg yolks

[crêpes flambé]

Prepare crêpe batter: Whisk eggs with sugar and salt until the mixture lightens. Sprinkle in the flour and then add milk (gradually, to prevent the formation of lumps). Let stand for 30 minutes.

Scrub citrus fruits under running water and remove rind with a vegetable peeler. Cut rind into fine strips and blanch for 3 minutes in boiling water.

Knead together butter, rinds, honey and half the Grand Marnier.

Grease a 12-inch nonstick frying pan with an oiled paper towel and make the crêpes: Pour on 1 small ladle of batter and spread it out quickly. Wait for 1 minute, then turn crêpe with a spatula and cook for 1–2 minutes. Transfer to a plate. Follow the same procedure to make about a dozen crêpes.

Before serving, spread a little of the citrus rind butter on the crêpes and fold into quarters. Return to the frying pan and place over low heat. Warm remaining Grand Marnier, flambé and pour over crêpes. Serve immediately.

Serves 4 (12 crêpes)
Prep time: 15 minutes
Standing time: 30 minutes
Cooking time:
about 35 minutes

For the crêpe batter:
2 eggs
3 tablespoons sugar
1 pinch salt
¾ cup flour
½ cup plus 2 tablespoons
   whole milk

½ orange
½ grapefruit
¼ cup softened butter
2 tablespoons orange
   blossom honey
¼ cup Grand Marnier,
   divided
1 tablespoon peanut oil

[pâte brisée*]

Sift flour. Cut butter into bits. Combine salt and flour, and add butter and rub dough between your hands to make a sort of sand.

Add 2 tablespoons cold water and quickly shape dough into a ball. Flatten it with the palm of your hand, form it into a ball again and refrigerate or let stand for 30 minutes in a cool place, covered, with a cloth before using.

*This rich dough is considered a "short pastry" and is used for crusts for both sweet and savory dishes. When using pâte brisée for a sweet dish, such as a fruit pie, add sugar to taste.

Serves 4
Prep time: 10 minutes
Standing time: 30 minutes

1⅓ cups flour
½ cup cold butter
   (about 4 ounces)
1 pinch salt

[pâte sablée*]

Serves 4
Prep time: 10 minutes
Standing time: 1 hour

10 tablespoons softened
    butter (1 stick plus
    2 tablespoons)
1⅔ cup sifted flour
1 egg
½ cup superfine sugar
1½ tablespoons vanilla
    sugar (see page 103)

Mix softened butter and sifted flour with the tips of your fingers, and then form a well in the center. Place egg and both types of sugar in the well and mix everything together rapidly to form a smooth, well-blended dough, but don't overmix.

Shape into a ball, and wrap in baking parchment or plastic wrap and chill for 1 hour before using.

*This delicate dough is also considered a "short pastry" and is used for tarts, cookies and small pastries.

[pâte feuilletée*]

Serves 4
Prep and standing time:
2 hours

9 ounces unsalted butter
    (2 sticks plus
    2 tablespoons)
1⅔ cups sifted flour
1 teaspoon salt
Flour for work surface

Prepare the dough: Melt 3 tablespoons of the butter, refrigerate the rest, and allow melted butter to cool. In a large bowl, mix flour and salt, then form a well. Pour ⅓ cup water into the center, and then gently mix the flour to prevent the formation of lumps.

Add melted butter, mix quickly to form a smooth, well-blended dough (mix just until all is combined) and shape into a ball. Refrigerate for 30 minutes.

Remove remaining butter from the refrigerator and place between 2 pieces of plastic wrap. Pound it with a rolling pin before flattening it into an 8 inch square.

Flour the work surface and roll out dough into a 12 inch square. Place butter in the center of the dough and fold edges over it to enclose. Flour the work surface again and place the dough on it. Roll out dough into a rectangle three times longer than it is wide. Bring each end of the rectangle over the middle, folding it into thirds, rotate it a quarter turn and roll it out again. Again fold the rectangle into thirds and let stand for 15 minutes.

Repeat this procedure (roll out, fold, turn) four more times, letting the dough stand again for 15 minutes after every 2 turns.

*This rich, buttery dough with hundreds of layers is also known as puff pastry.

[spiced pears with wine]

Scrub orange under running water, then remove half of the rind and cut the rind into fine strips. Squeeze juice from half of the orange. Split vanilla bean lengthwise.

In a large saucepan, heat red wine, orange juice, orange rind, vanilla bean, brown sugar and spices.

Carefully peel pears, and then add to spiced wine. Cover and boil for about 5 minutes and let cool.

Just before serving, remove pears from the liquid. Reduce the liquid until it becomes syrupy. Then pour it over the fruit and serve immediately.

Serves 4
Prep time: 20 minutes
Cooking time: 30 minutes

1 orange
1 vanilla bean
4 cups red wine
1⅓ cups brown sugar
1 stick cinnamon
1 generous pinch freshly
   grated nutmeg
4 firm pears, barely ripe
   (such as comice)

For vanilla sugar:
2 vanilla beans (bourbon
   vamilla beans, if available)
3 cups granulated sugar
3 cups brown sugar

For the cinnamon sugar:
3 tablespoons
   ground cinnamon
2 pound brown sugar
1 large stick cinnamon

[flavored sugars]

Vanilla sugar: Split vanilla beans in half lengthwise. Place in a jar with a lid. Combine two types of sugar and pour over vanilla beans. Close the jar.

Cinnamon sugar: Combine the ground cinnamon and brown sugar. Pour into a jar with a lid, and add cinnamon stick and close the jar.

Wait 1 week before using these flavored sugars, and use in milk products or on fruit salads.

[baked apples with cinnamon and vanilla]

Serves 4
Prep time: 10 minutes
Cooking time: 45 minutes

4 large tart apples
3 tablespoons butter
3 tablespoons granulated
   sugar, divided
1 tablespoon ground
   cinnamon
2 vanilla beans (bourbon
   vamilla beans, if available)
Cremè anglaise
   (see page 112)

Preheat oven to 350°F. Wash, dry and core apples. Place in a gratin dish.

Work butter into a paste together with half the sugar and the cinnamon. Stuff each apple with this flavored butter and ½ vanilla bean split lengthwise. Sprinkle with the remaining sugar and place in the oven.

Bake for about 45 minutes until the apples are tender. Test doneness by piercing apples with the tip of a knife.

Serve apples while warm garnished with very cold crème anglaise.

[floating islands]

Serves 4
Prep time: 25 minutes
Refrigeration time:
30 minutes
Cooking time: 10 minutes

4 eggs, divided (yolks for
   crème anglaise; whites
   for "islands")
1 recipe crème anglaise
   (see page 112), using:
1¼ cup whole milk
1 bean vanilla bean
   (bourbon vanilla bean,
   if available)
⅔ cup sugar, divided
1 pinch salt

For the caramel:
¼ cup sugar
Dash fresh lemon juice
   (about ⅛ teaspoon)

Break eggs and separate whites from yolks. Prepare crème anglaise according to the recipe on page 112, using the 4 egg yolks, milk, vanilla bean and ¼ cup of the sugar. Pour crème anglaise into a pie plate or serving dish (about 10 inches) with sides and allow to cool a bit.

Add salt to egg whites and beat into soft peaks. Add the remaining sugar and beat egg whites into stiff peaks. Take large tablespoons of egg white and poach two at a time in simmering water. Poach for about 2 minutes, gently turning them to cook on all sides. Lift from water and strain. Place on top of créme anglaise and refrigerate until caramel is done.*

When you put the dessert in the refrigerator to chill, prepare the caramel: In a heavy saucepan, heat the sugar, 1 tablespoon water and lemon juice. As soon as it turns light brown, drizzle caramel in very thin threads on top of the egg whites and crème anglaise. Serve immediately.

*May be made ahead to this point and kept, covered, in refrigerator for several hours.

If you make a thicker crumble, bake it longer at a lower temperature. These desserts are not at all temperamental and can stand a little stewing. Adding ground almonds to the dough will produce a truly regal crumble.

[apple-pear crumble with ginger]

In a bowl, combine flour, granulated sugar, ginger and salt. Add very cold butter, cut into bits. Work the mixture by rubbing it between your hands until it resembles coarse sand. Refrigerate.

Preheat oven to 400°F.

Peel fruit, cut into small pieces and transfer to 4 individual gratin dishes with 7 inch diameters (or 1 large dish). Remove crumble dough from refrigerator and sprinkle over fruit. Bake for about 15 minutes in the oven until the crumble is golden. Finish cooking by placing briefly under the broiler.

Serve warm topped with a spoonful of crème fraîche. If you make this dessert in one large dish, double the cooking time.

Serves 4
Prep time: 15 minutes
Cooking time: 15 minutes

⅔ cup flour
½ cup granulated sugar
3 pinches ground ginger
1 pinch salt
8 tablespoons cold butter
   (1 stick)
3 ripe firm pears
   (such as comice)
2 tart apples
½ cup crème fraîche

[baba au rhum]

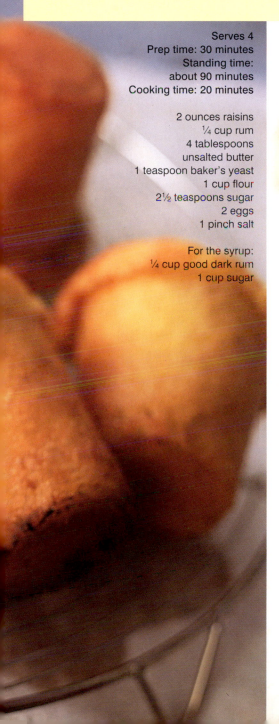

Serves 4
Prep time: 30 minutes
Standing time:
about 90 minutes
Cooking time: 20 minutes

2 ounces raisins
¼ cup rum
4 tablespoons
unsalted butter
1 teaspoon baker's yeast
1 cup flour
2½ teaspoons sugar
2 eggs
1 pinch salt

For the syrup:
¼ cup good dark rum
1 cup sugar

Soak raisins in rum. Remove butter from refrigerator.

Mix yeast with 3 tablespoons warm water. Place flour in a large bowl, form a well in the center of the flour and pour in sugar, 1 egg, salt and watered-down yeast. Work the mixture with a spatula until it becomes elastic (about 8 minutes). Add the second egg, while continuing to work the dough. Then add 2 tablespoons of the softened butter and the strained raisins. Let dough rise for 30 minutes in the bowl.

Butter 8 baba molds (or other small individual baking molds or dishes). Punch down the dough, then transfer it to the molds and let rise for another 60 minutes in a warm place.

Preheat oven to 400°F

When the dough completely fills the molds, bake for about 20 minutes in the oven. Test doneness by piercing the babas with the tip of a knife. The blade should come out clean.

Prepare the syrup by boiling ⅓ cup water with dark rum and sugar.

Remove babas from molds, place on a cake rack set on top of a dish, and moisten with the syrup. Place them in a shallow dish and baste them periodically with the sauce that runs off.

Serve plain or garnished with preserved fruit and whipped cream.

You can also make one large baba in a nonstick savarin or other ring mold with a 10 inch diameter. In this case, bake for an additional 10 minutes.

[apple caramel tart with butter]

Serves 4
Prep time: 20 minutes
Cooking time: 40 minutes

3 large tart apples
Flour for the work surface
12 ounces puff pastry
  dough (about ¾ of the
  recipe on page 101)
2 tablespoons butter

For the caramel:
½ cup sugar
½ cup crème fraîche
1½ tablespoons butter

Peel and core apples and cut into thin slices. On a floured work surface, roll out puff pastry dough into a round or square of about 15 inches across. Set in a tin about 12 inches across. Preheat oven to 400°F.

Arrange apples on the dough, sprinkle with butter cut into bits and bake in the oven for 30 to 40 minutes.

Prepare the caramel: In a small saucepan, melt sugar over low heat. In another saucepan, heat crème fraîche. When the sugar takes on a nice caramel color, add crème fraîche and, while stirring constantly, cook until it becomes a toffee. Pour into a bowl and gently fold in butter. Let cool.

When the tart is done, take it out of the oven. Remove it from the tin and place on a cake rack. Let it cool a little before pouring on the caramel. Serve immediately.

[grandma alice's tart dough]

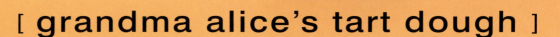

Makes 12 ounces dough
Prep time: 5 minutes

8 tablespoons butter
  (1 stick)
1 cup flour
¼ cup cornstarch
1 teaspoon yeast
1 pinch fine salt
1 egg

Melt butter over low heat; allow to cool. **C**ombine flour, cornstarch, yeast and salt. Add egg and whisk energetically with a fork to form a sort of "sand." Preheat oven to 350°F.

Add melted butter and work rapidly with a wooden spoon to shape dough into a ball. Using the flat of your hand, spread out immediately in a tin 15 inches across. Cover with fruit or some kind of savory mixture and bake for about 30 minutes in a hot oven.

You can keep this dough in the refrigerator for 2 days, rolled out and covered with plastic wrap (this will only make the tart better).

Boil milk with vanilla bean split in half lengthwise. Cover and let steep for 10 minutes. Then remove vanilla bean.

In the meantime, beat egg yolks and sugar until mixture lightens. Gradually add flavored milk, mix and transfer to a heavy saucepan. Simmer for 15 minutes over very low heat, while stirring constantly, until the cream thickens and coats a spoon. Immediately pour into a large bowl and let cool.

Never allow the custard to boil because this would cause the egg yolks to congeal and form lumps.

Serves 4
Prep time: 10 minutes
Cooking time:
about 15 minutes

1¼ cups whole milk
1 vanilla bean (bourbon
   vanilla bean, if available)
4 egg yolks
¼ cup sugar

[crème anglaise]
custard sauce

The Tart of the Demoiselles Tatin is one of several legendary dishes that are said to be the result of an error.

According to the story, one of the sisters accidentally

turned the tart upside-down and, to keep from wasting it, finished baking it as it was. The result was worth taking

the chance. As for crème brûlée, which began to appear on bistro menus in the 1980s, it is thought to come from either Catalonia or the kitchens of Oxford University.

[tarte tatin with pears]

Serves 4
Prep time: 15 minutes
Cooking time: 30 minutes

3 large firm pears
   (such as comice)
Flour for work surface
½ recipe puff pastry (page
   101 or ⅔ recipe shortcrust
   pastry dough, page 100;
   about 8 ounce pastry,
   if purchased)
½ cup sugar
1 pinch ground cardamom
1 pinch ground cinnamon
⅓ cup butter
⅓ cup cinnamon sugar
   (see page 103)
⅓ cup whipping cream

Peel pears and cut into thin slices. Flour a work surface and roll out dough into a round 12 inches across.

Preheat oven to 400°F. Combine sugar and spices. Slowly melt butter in a nonstick tin 11 inches across and 2–3 inches high. Sprinkle with cinnamon sugar (reserving 2 tablespoons) and arrange pear slices on top, fitting them tightly together. Sprinkle with the remaining cinnamon sugar and bake for 10 minutes until fruit is barely caramelized. Let cool.

In the meantime, lightly whip cream and refrigerate.

Pierce the pastry dough several times with a fork and gently lay it over the pears. Tuck the edges into the tin and place in the oven. Bake for 15 minutes, then lower temperature to 350°F and bake for another 5 minutes.

Remove tart from the tin while it is still hot, and serve with the whipped cream.

[crème brûlée with vanilla]

Serves 4
Prep time: 30 minutes
Cooking time:
20–30 minutes
Refrigeration time:
at least 1 hour

⅓ cup whole milk
1¼ cups half-and-half
2 vanilla beans (bourbon
   vanilla beans, if available)
7 egg yolks
½ cup granulated sugar
¼ cup brown sugar

Bring milk and half-and-half to a boil. Add vanilla beans split in half lengthwise. Remove from heat, cover and let steep for 30 minutes.

Preheat oven to 300°F. Beat egg yolks and granulated sugar, then add vanilla milk. Stir and pour through a chinois or fine mesh strainer.

Transfer custard to 4 ramekins or small ceramic gratin dishes, place in a bain-marie (see page 18) and bake on the center rack of the oven for 20–30 minutes. Mixture should be set, but still wobble a little in the center.

Let custard cool thoroughly, then refrigerate. Just before serving, sprinkle with a thin layer of brown sugar and place under the broiler for a few moments.

Serves 4
Prep time: 30 minutes
Cooking time: 5–7 minutes

3½ ounces semi-sweet
  baking chocolate squares
6 tablespoons butter
⅓ cup sugar
4 eggs
2 teaspoons cornstarch
1 pinch salt
2 tablespoons very
  strong coffee

[rich mocha cake]

Coarsely chop or grate chocolate and melt slowly in a double boiler. Place 5 tablespoons of the butter on top so it melts at the same time as the chocolate. Use the rest of the butter to grease 4 high-sided ceramic ramekins or 4 aluminum tins and sprinkle with 2 tablespoons of the sugar. **B**reak eggs and separate whites from yolks. Whisk yolks with the remaining sugar until mixture lightens and then add cornstarch. Add salt to whites and beat into stiff peaks. Combine chocolate and melted butter. Let cool, then add egg yolks and finally the coffee (do not mix together too thoroughly). Gently fold into the stiff egg whites and transfer to tins. **P**reheat oven to 400°F. Bake cakes for 5–7 minutes in aluminum tins or 10 minutes in ceramic dishes. Carefully turn out of tins onto separate plates and serve warm.

[glossary]

Basil: This herb has a sunny flavor but is really only tasty and available at markets when the weather is fair. To preserve it throughout the gray months, chop it coarsely, cover it with olive oil and freeze it in small containers.

Caraway: This spice is often confused with cumin, which has a very different taste. Caraway is very common in Central and Eastern European cuisine where it is used to flavor bread and pastries.

Cardamom: This spice, which is very common in India and the Middle East, comes in the form of pods filled with seeds. Three varieties are available: green, white and brown.

Garlic: Can be kept for several months in a dry place but starts to sprout after 3 months. It's better to remove any sprouts from the cloves before eating them cooked or raw. They will then be easier to digest.

Herbs: Herbs contribute a divine aroma to the simplest of dishes. If you use them in a hot dish, don't add them until the very end or else they'll lose their flavor. Put them in at the last possible moment.

Parmesan: When authentic, this Italian cheese made from cow's milk carries the label "Parmigiano-Reggiano." In this case, it is aged at least one year before being sold. It's best to grate it just before using. Avoid buying pre-packaged, grated Parmesan because the quality is largely mediocre and has little in common with this king of cheeses.

Preserved lemons: These come in two types: Lemons candied in sugar, the rinds of which are used to flavor cakes and rice pudding, and lemons preserved in brine, used in Moroccan dishes and a perfect accompaniment to veal and lamb. They are sold in bulk or by the jar at oriental markets and will keep for several months in the refrigerator.

Saffron: This spice is highly prized and extremely expensive. It comes in the form of small dark-red threads derived from the stamens and pistils of a crocus. It is sold in small jars and serves to flavor bouillabaisse, paella, risotto, etc..

Spices: Spices are best purchased "whole" in the form of seeds or sticks rather than pre-ground. This allows them to retain their full flavor over a longer period of time. You can then grate or grind them when you're ready to use them.

Sugar: Several varieties of sugar are available. The best is derived from sugar cane rather than from sugar beets. Sugar comes in various flavors and textures, depending on the degree to which it has been refined. Don't hesitate to keep several types on hand, such as brown, molasses, raw sugar, etc.

Wonton skins: These small squares of fresh dough made from eggs are used for making Chinese ravioli and are sold in the refrigerated sections of Asian markets. If necessary, you can substitute fresh lasagna noodle dough sold by Italian caterers.

glossary

[index]

Published originally under the title Bistrot, ©2000 HACHETTE LIVRE (Hachette Pratique)

English translation for the U.S. market ©2001, Silverback Books, Inc.

Managing editors: Suyapa Audigier & Brigitte Éveno

Project editor: Lisa M. Tooker

Food editor: Terri Pischoff Wuerthner, CCP

Artwork and creation: Guylaine & Christophe Moi

Production: Nathalie Lautout & Patty Holden

Assistant editor: Sophie Brissaud

Editorial office: Sylvie Gauthier

Object photography: Matthieu Csech

Cover photo: Editing / J. P. Bajard

Photos: Page 10 The Image Bank / Marvin E. Newman, page 32 Agence Ana / J. du Sorbet, page 52 Editing / J. P. Bajard, page 74 Tony Stone Images / Martine Mouchy, page 96 Tony Stone Images / Joe Cornish

Printed and bound in Singapore.

ISBN : 1930603-51-7